BEIJING
THE CITY AT A GLANCE

Sanlitun
The embassy quarter is gentrifying fast, thanks to sophisticated arrivals such as The Opposite House (see p022) and Sanlitun Village.
See Neighbourhoods

Houhai
Beijing's bustling lakes are still an entertaining place for a sundowner and a tour on the water.
See p037

Jingshan Park
Climb the manmade hill in this popular park, once an imperial garden, for sweeping vistas.
Jingshan Qianjie

Forbidden City
The last emperor left in 1924, leaving 8,700 rooms in mothballs. Thanks to the Olympics and restorers, more areas are now open to view.
See p012

CCTV Building
Despite the best intentions of the architects, this CBD landmark has been beset by problems.
See p010

Wangfujing
Flash malls are replacing the hutongs around Beijing's long-standing shopping zone. At least the dim sum is good at Lei Garden (T 8522 1212).

NCPA
Paul Andreu's once-divisive design has pro to be a boon for the performing arts.
See p068

Chairman Mao Memorial Hall
The Great Helmsman had asked to be crema but thanks to his hangers-on his embalmed corpse lies in state in a crystal coffin.
See p066

D1713866

INTRODUCTION

THE CHANGING FACE OF THE URBAN SCENE

Beijing is, without doubt, one of the fastest-changing cities in the world. But then what else would you expect from the capital of the next would-be global superpower? A generation-defining transformation is taking place here – one that shifted to warp speed in the run-up to the 2008 Olympics and has continued apace long after the circus has moved on. The zeal and hunger to modernise that Beijing displayed to the world that year remain. All eyes are now on China, and rightly so. Whether your focus is on economics, politics or culture, the signs point to a growing assertiveness. Yet the country's roaring cities and high-flying corporations belie a messier underside (the debt bubbles of the construction boom; the blight of the environment and an insatiable need for energy), which is not lost on China's unruly netizenry, and a government painfully trying to chart a more sustainable future course.

Beijing is the beating heart of the beast. Sure, its southern rival Shanghai may be the glitzy financial centre, but there's something addictive about the capital. Smooth and pretty it ain't, but the place has a rich culture and a monumental spirit, from its ancient imperial grandeur to its contemporary starchitecture. While the city boggles the mind with its many contradictions, it remains a hotpot of possibilities. This is where the nation's creatives are drawn for inspiration, by the impalpable but real feeling that here, today, something is happening.

ESSENTIAL INFO

FACTS, FIGURES AND USEFUL ADDRESSES

TOURIST OFFICE
269 Wangfujing Dajie
T 8511 0468
www.visitbeijing.com.cn

TRANSPORT
Car hire
Beijing Top-A Car Service
T 6438 1634
Public transport
Beijing Subway
www.bjsubway.com/ens/index.html
The subway runs from around 5am-11pm
Taxis
Beijing Taxi Dispatch Centre
T 6837 3399
Cabs can also be hailed on the street

EMERGENCY SERVICES
Ambulance
T 120
Fire
T 119
Police
T 110
24-hour pharmacy
Suite 105
Wing 1
Kunsha Dasha
16 Xinyuanli
T 6462 9112
www.internationalsos.com

EMBASSIES
British Embassy
11 Guanghua Lu
T 5192 4000
www.ukinchina.fco.gov.uk
US Embassy
55 Anjialou Lu
T 8531 3000
beijing.usembassy-china.org.cn

MONEY
American Express
T 6505 2228
www.americanexpress.com

POSTAL SERVICES
Post office
3 Gongti Beilu
T 6416 8214
Shipping
UPS
1 Jianguomenwaidajie
T 6505 5005

BOOKS
Country Driving: A Chinese Road Trip
by Peter Hessler (Canongate Books)
The Last Days of Old Beijing: Life in the Vanishing Backstreets of a City Transformed by Michael Meyer
(Walker & Co)
Nine Lives: The Birth of Avant-Garde Art in New China by Karen Smith (Timezone 8)

WEBSITES
Art/design
www.review.redboxstudio.cn
Newspapers
www.chinadaily.com.cn
www.globaltimes.cn

COST OF LIVING
Taxi from BCI Airport to city centre
RMB80 (including RMB10 toll)
Cappuccino
RMB30
Packet of cigarettes
RMB10
Daily newspaper
RMB1.5
Bottle of champagne
RMB750

BEIJING
Area
16,410 sq km
Population
20 million
Currency
Renminbi
Telephone codes
China: 86
Beijing: 10
Time
GMT +8

CHINA

○ Sapporo
○ Tokyo
○ Osaka
□ Beijing
● Shanghai
○ Hong Kong
○ Mumbai ○ Kolkata

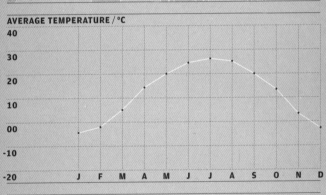

AVERAGE TEMPERATURE / °C

40												
30												
20												
10												
00												
-10												
-20	J	F	M	A	M	J	J	A	S	O	N	D

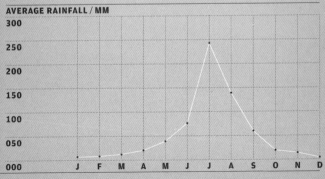

AVERAGE RAINFALL / MM

300												
250												
200												
150												
100												
050												
000	J	F	M	A	M	J	J	A	S	O	N	D

NEIGHBOURHOODS

THE AREAS YOU NEED TO KNOW AND WHY

To help you navigate the city, we've chosen the most interesting districts (see below and the map inside the back cover) and colour-coded our featured venues, according to their location; those venues that are outside these areas are not coloured.

EAST SIDE

OMA's HQ for the state broadcaster, CCTV (see p010), has redrawn the landscape of Beijing's CBD, while construction along the East Third Ring Road continues to yield a mountain range of glass-and-steel skyscrapers. Ghettoes of quietude can be found in the old embassy area, though perhaps not in the Russian neighbourhood around Yabao Lu. Climb the rockery in the perfectly manicured Ritan Park for a great view of Chaoyang business district.

UNIVERSITIES

Liang Sicheng, the founder of China's leading school of architecture at Tsinghua University, begged Mao to save the walls of the old city and build a new administrative centre to its north-west. Alas, he and his Soviet advisers declined. But the digital economy is making up for Mao's miscue. The area is no longer home to punks and poor scholars but research institutes, internet cafés and towers of tech geeks.

TIANANMEN

The geographical and historical centre of the city is a hopscotch through the yin and yang of modern China's past. Stay at The Emperor (see p028) to the east of the Forbidden City (see p012), whose doors open daily, unlike those of the adjacent Communist Party HQ Zhongnanhai. Next to the Great Hall of the People (see p064), a big classical box, is Paul Andreu's NCPA (see p068) – a futuristic bubble.

GULOU

Sadly, a whole chunk of this part of the old city has fallen prey to the wrecking ball and rents have surged throughout many of the hutongs, threatening the bohemian equilibrium of the area. But the hipsters remain, which means an abundance of trendy shops, bars and restaurants. The action is centred around the Bell Tower (Gulou Xidajie), Gulou Dongdajie, where you'll find Paper (see p042), and Nanluoguxiang.

OLD CITY

Once home to concubines, warlords and the literati, the labyrinthine blocks surrounding the emperor's old 'hood are prime real estate once again. In the interim, the area was ravaged by Maoist collectivisation and Olympic-driven modernisation. Properties like Hotel Côté Cour (see p026) are hidden gems amid the ersatz malls. Visit the Temple of Heaven (see p033) for imperial-era inspiration.

SANLITUN

The Hydra of Beijing nightlife. Expats christened the leafy embassy zone with a few pubs in the early 1990s and beloved hangouts were soon born on Sanlitun Nanlu. Modern complexes like Sanlitun Village have shifted the area upmarket, bringing some comfort and class, and limiting the colourful seediness to a single back alley. Clubs and drinking dens still flourish around the Workers' Stadium.

LANDMARKS
THE SHAPE OF THE CITY SKYLINE

Credit the Mongols, who under Kublai Khan founded the Yuan dynasty (1271-1368), for Beijing's masterplan. It called for the 'Great Capital' to be laid out on a symmetrical grid with a central axis bisecting the imperial palace. The early Ming emperors erected the <u>Forbidden City</u> (see p012) at the core, and the Qing dynasty Manchus kept that schema intact. Not so Mao's planners, who tore down the city wall to build the Second Ring Road. This set the pattern of concentric ring roads that has rippled outwards ever since. Beijing's layout – as incomprehensible as it may appear on the ground – is self-explanatory. The city is its own compass.

Today, the north is best known for the Olympic Green and its modern landmarks – the National Stadium (see p014) and the National Aquatics Center (11 Tianchen Donglu, T 8437 8086), aka the Water Cube – whereas the south is dominated by the imperial-era <u>Temple of Heaven</u> (see p033). Campus life is confined mostly to the north-west, with corporate affairs mostly to the east. The latter is the closest to what could be called downtown, and includes a CBD around the <u>CCTV Building</u> (overleaf) and <u>China World Trade Center</u> (1 Jianguomenwai Dajie, T 6505 2288).

If only getting around the capital was so simple. Beijing's huge, kilometre-square blocks make most districts unwalkable, although travel has been improved significantly by the expanding subway. *For full addresses, see Resources.*

CCTV Building

Ole Scheeren and Rem Koolhaas' building for China's state-run television network, CCTV, has redefined the look of the city's fast-rising CBD. There is perhaps no better representation of the ambition of 21st-century Beijing than this $1.2bn loop of glass and steel, popularly nicknamed the 'big underpants'. Rather than join an unthinking race up to the heavens, the structure features two leaning towers: one used for broadcasting, the other for research and education — linked on the ground and, giddily, at the top, in a space reserved for management. The complex has not been without its problems. Engineers Arup broke ground in 2004, although the CCTV HQ will only become fully operational in 2011, having laid vacant after an unauthorised fireworks display engulfed OMA's adjacent hotel and cultural centre in flames in 2009. *East Third Ring Road/Guanghua Lu*

Forbidden City

Chairman Mao faced south, just as any emperor of yore would have done, on declaring his dominion from the Forbidden City's Gate of Heavenly Peace in 1949. His portrait now hangs above the main entrance, but superstition, it is said, stopped him from ever setting foot inside the 720,000 sq m complex. The Son of Heaven's old digs, which symbolically sit directly on the city's central axis, sparkle under a dusting of snow and at night; especially the ghostly moat (pictured) at the Wumen gate. The building was commissioned in 1406. The bricks are made of white lime and glutinous rice, and there are egg whites in the cement. The walls of the 'Purple Forbidden City', as it is also known, are 'pig's-liver red'. *North of Tiananmen Square, T 8500 7421, www.dpm.org.cn*

National Stadium

The Mongol conquerors placed their northern gate about here. Seven centuries on, Herzog & de Meuron landed the Olympic stadium bid with its 'Bird's Nest', partly thanks to input from Beijing art luminary Ai Weiwei, who later cursed the creation in a tirade against the regime. The 91,000-seat arena swallowed up some $500.7m in its construction, but no one was counting the cost when the structure wowed the world. Since then, however, there have been questions over what to do with it – tourism revenue struggles to cover the $22m annual operating costs. Now, so long as it pays, anything goes – from a Jackie Chan concert to the Italian football Super Cup and a winter sports park with ski slopes.
Olympic Green, T 8437 3008

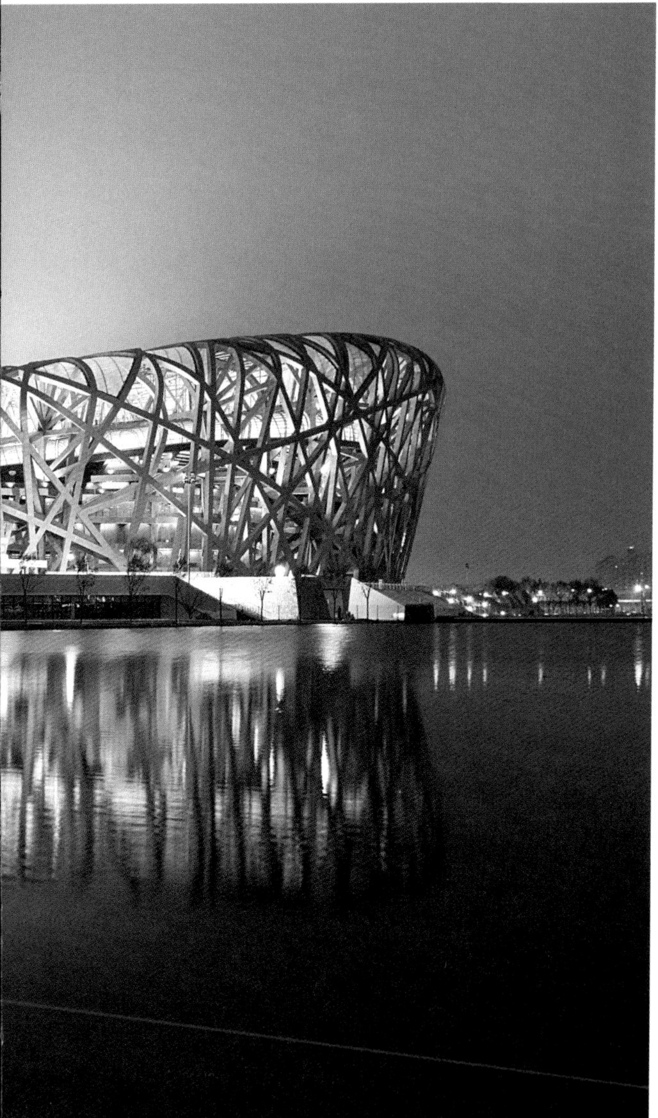

HOTELS
WHERE TO STAY AND WHICH ROOMS TO BOOK

The first international five-star hotel to open in Beijing was The Great Wall Sheraton (10 Dongsanhuan Beilu, T 6590 5566), in 1984. The property brought a sense of modernity to an emerging market, principally thanks to its use of mirrored-glass cladding. While its exterior may seem unsophisticated today, it remains a fitting symbol of the start of Beijing's architectural overhaul.

Things have come a long way. Now, and especially after the glut of hotels developed for the Olympics, visitors can take their pick of the luxury chains. Many can be found along the main boulevard of Chang'an or the coaxial Jianguomenwai Dajie, stretching from the CBD to Tiananmen Square – perfect for both business and sightseeing. The downside is that the surroundings can feel impersonal, due to the area's somewhat inhuman scale.

Luckily, for those who prefer something more individual, there has also been an influx of boutique hotels, in locations across the city. The trend began in 2006, with the arrival of Studio Pei-Zhu's Hotel Kapok (16 Donghuamen Dajie, T 6525 9988) and has been strengthened by additions such as Yi House (see p020), The Emperor (see p028), 3+1 Bedrooms (see p031) and the playful Hotel G (A7 Gongti Xilu, T 6552 3600). Then, of course, there's The Opposite House (see p022), which – all hyperbole aside – has taken the Beijing hotel scene to an entirely new level.

For full addresses and room rates, see Resources.

Aman at Summer Palace

Set next to the east gate of the Summer Palace (T 6288 1144), one of the city's most beautiful sites, Aman's impressive resort takes inspiration from its neighbour. Suites, such as the Imperial (above), surround an internal courtyard (overleaf) and dwellings sumptuously updated from when they were occupied by guests of the Dowager Empress Cixi at the end of the 19th century. Designed by Jaya Ibrahim with Jean-Michel Gathy, the hotel boasts a resident calligrapher, a library and several elegant courtyard restaurants; try the Japanese eaterie Naoki. There's also a private entrance to the Summer Palace. A word of warning: this is not the most convenient option if you need to travel across the city to the CBD.
1 Gongmenqianjie, T 5987 9999, www.amanresorts.com

Courtyard, Aman at Summer Palace

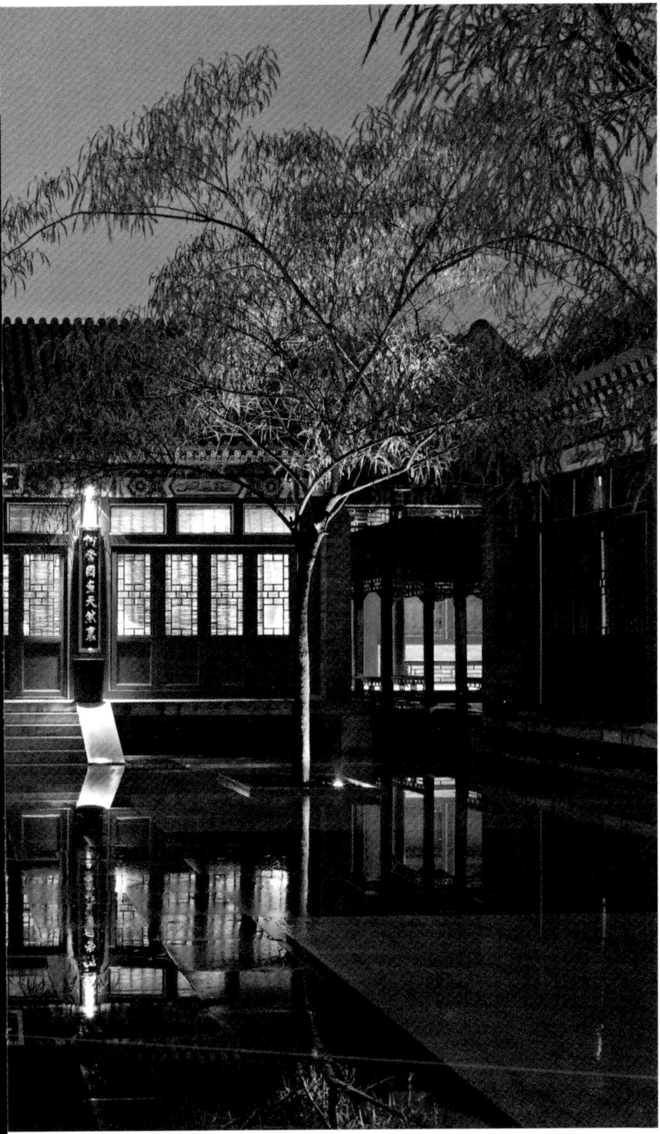

Yi House

Thanks to Shauna Liu, who made her name with Hotel Côté Cour (see p026), the Dashanzi Art District now offers accommodation worthy of its artistic and architectural heritage. Yi House was carved out of an old crystal factory and comprises 30 rooms, including the Deluxe Suites (above), each with a different take on the hotel's aesthetic: a mix of modern Chinese art (photographs by Beijing-based Chi Peng hang in several of the rooms), old-world Asia and art deco. If you want to splash out, plump for the Emperor Suite (left), which uses materials such as white crystal and jade from Sichuan in the bathroom. The in-house Fennel Restaurant serves good Mediterranean cuisine.
*2 Jiuxianqiao Lu, T 6436 1818,
www.yi-house.com*

The Opposite House
Japanese architect Kengo Kuma's
99-room boutique hotel – a modernist
green-glass cube in Sanlitun – is in a
class of its own in Beijing. The slate and
natural timbers used in the airy studios
and suites (Penthouse, pictured) give
it the feel of a tranquil urban retreat.
Don't forego a soak in your solid oak tub.
11 Sanlitun Lu, T 6417 6688,
www.theoppositehouse.com

Raffles Hotel

After several austere updates in the 1950s, 1970s and 1990s, this hotel reopened as part of the Raffles group in 2006. The original 1917 façade, a blend of French and oriental influences, was preserved, along with the arches, inlaid stone in the lobby and wooden floor in the Writers Bar, where Zhou Enlai is said to have entertained Ho Chi Minh. Fashion prince Benny Ong clad the bellhops and interior designer Grace Soh dressed up the rooms. Only the veneer of the floors and furniture leaves the place still feeling a bit new. Opt for four-poster elegance in a Landmark Suite or one of the nine Personality Suites (above). Savour modern French cuisine at in-house restaurant Jaan and sip a Singapore Sling in the Writers Bar. *33 Dongchang'anjie, T 6526 3388, www.beijing.raffles.com*

China World Hotel

During the 1990s, the vermilion-and-gold foyer (above) of this Shangri-La hotel was the city's power lobby. Others have come along since, but after a 2003 makeover, the space retained its incomparable sense of drama. Set within the China World Trade Centre (CWTC), the hotel attracts dignitaries and captains of industry. The downstairs shopping mall features a few idiosyncratic boutiques, while the updated rooms, such as the Beijing Suite, are dotted with contemporary Asian art. The remodelled dining room is much brighter than most. The hotel and CWTC Tower 1 were constructed during the late 1980s, and with their subtle curves, the brown glass edifices are far more palatable than many that have popped up since.
*1 Jianguomenwai Dajie, T 6505 2266,
www.shangri-la.com*

Hotel Côté Cour
Can Beijing have too many courtyard
hotels? If they're all as charming as Hotel
Côté Cour, then no, especially as the old
hutongs where these boutique properties
are found are in danger of being lost for
ever. There are just 14 rooms, including
the Superior Suite (opposite), surrounding
a tranquil courtyard (above), so your stay
here will be a peaceful one. The interiors
are all about classical Chinese chic –
ancient brick floors, sumptuous silks
and Tibetan rugs – while the main gate
embraces the ancient traditions of this
500-year-old site with two guardian
lion statues and a screen wall said
to protect the building from evil spirits.
The hotel can be a bit tricky to find,
but it's well worth the effort for a taste
of a China being swallowed up by the
unstoppable drive for modernisation.
70 Yanyue Hutong, T 6523 7981,
www.hotelcotecourbj.com

The Emperor

If you want to be near the geographical centre of the city, book one of the 55 rooms at this contemporary hotel. Hidden away down a hutong to the east of the Forbidden City (see p012), the exterior of what used to be the drab premises of the Tsinghua University alumni association belies the slick hotel within – all flowing curves and a clever use of colour. The interiors are courtesy of design studio Graft, who gave each floor a different scheme. Our top choice is the 68.5 sq m Emperor Suite (opposite). The rooftop bar, Yin, with its wooden decking and outdoor jacuzzi (above), has an unbeatable view, especially at sunset, stretching from Jingshan Park to the Forbidden City. Check it out whether you're staying here or not. *33 Qiheloujie, T 6526 5566, www.theemperor.com.cn*

Red Capital Residence

This jocularly named hospitality brand is the brainchild of US China aficionado Laurence Brahm. He started with the Red Capital Club (T 8401 6152), a home-style supper club, and has also opened a retreat, the Red Capital Ranch (T 8401 8886). All three are receptacles for his collection of curios from the corridors of Communist Party power, as seen in the Capital Residence's reception room (above). If nostalgia means more to you than creature comforts, this centuries-old courtyard hotel is worth a sleepover. The hotel's five rooms are dedicated to writers – Mao's embedded Long March biographer Edgar Snow and the doctor-cum-novelist Han Suyin – concubines, and, of course, to the Chairman himself. *9 Dongsi Liutiao, T 8403 5308, www.redcapitalclub.com.cn*

3+1 Bedrooms

There are only three rooms and one suite, the Jade (above), at this hip hutong hideaway from Malaysian entrepreneur Cho Chong Gee, who also owns Paper (see p042), and two other Dongcheng venues. Tucked down an alley near the Drum Tower, behind a steel door, the minimalist 3+1 has a stark white interior punctuated by areas of exposed concrete. Each room also has its own bamboo-strewn patio. The reception doubles as a bar and Malaysian food can be ordered in from Gee's Café Sambal (T 6400 4875), while the roof terrace is a great place to scan the skyline. Or stroll to another chilled-out venue in his empire in the same hutong, Bed Tapas & Bar (T 8400 1554) – a popular courtyard hideout with *kang*-style beds. *17 Zhangwang Hutong, off Jiugulou Dajie, T 6404 7030, www.3plus1bedrooms.com*

24 HOURS

SEE THE BEST OF THE CITY IN JUST ONE DAY

Beijing is a historic capital where the sites are all too often poorly explained, while park life is frequently overlooked in a city that is as unrelentingly urban as they come. Jingshan, a former imperial garden north of the Forbidden City (see p012), has a hill worth scaling for lovely early-morning views, while at the same time of day, the Temple of Heaven (opposite) makes for the least tourist-clogged introduction to the dynastic splendours of the Old City.

Beijing's intellectual and art scenes are as critical to its quest for an international identity as Zhongnanhai – the State Council and Communist Party HQ – is to its pursuit of power. Before the Olympics, it was the avant-garde that breathed credibility back into this hugely creative city. Serious aficionados should travel to Caochangdi, Ai Weiwei's art enclave on the north-east outskirts of the city. Sadly, the area is slated for demolition so catch it while you can. Or head to Dashanzi (see p034), a little overrun these days but worth a visit if this is your first time in Beijing.

This isn't much of a walking city, but there are parts that you can happily cover on foot. Dali Courtyard (see p052) is a great place to have lunch before embarking on an afternoon wander around the hutongs of Gulou (see p036) and Houhai (see p037). In the evening, feast on Peking duck, the local speciality. Duck de Chine (see p038) is the best-looking place to try it.

For full addresses, see Resources.

07.30 Temple of Heaven

Built in the 15th century, at the same time as the Forbidden City (see p012), this was where the Chinese emperors came to make sacrifices and pray for prosperity. The main temple, the Hall of Prayer for Good Harvests (above), with its triple-eaved blue tiled roof, is particularly striking, and something of an architectural marvel. The 38m-tall wooden building was constructed without the use of a single nail and the walls carry no weight; the load is transferred instead to the 28 columns. Most of the key sites in the complex open at 8am, although the 273-hectare park can be entered from 6am, when it comes alive with Beijing's older residents exercising, singing and playing cards or mah-jong. *Tiantan Gongyuan, T 6702 8866, en.tiantanpark.com*

11.00 Dashanzi Art District

It was here that Beijing's avant-garde first stumbled on a post-industrial 'promised land', with the Maoist slogans on the walls providing a powerfully gimmicky context. The area was soon dubbed 798, after the Bauhaus-style 798 Factory plant at its core, now the 798 Space exhibition centre. Today, it's a hub of cafés and art galleries, including the influential UCCA (above), founded by Belgian collectors and philanthropists Guy and Myriam Ullens. Opened in November 2007, UCCA occupies several buildings, making it one of the largest art complexes in the Dashanzi area. Now run as a non-profit organisation, it focuses on international and Chinese artists, such as Beijing-based Li Songsong (*Pig Years*, above).
4 Jiuxianqiao Lu, Dashanzi Art District, T 8459 9269, www.ucca.org.cn

李松松
LI SONGSONG

15.00 Hutong tour

The hutongs, Beijing's folk ecosystem of alleyways, are slowly dying. Planners said they were protecting some of the old neighbourhoods within the Second Ring Road when the Olympics accelerated urban-renewal efforts, but preservation is often code for prettification: relics are saved but traditional homes are gutted. Some hutong redevelopments, such as the Disneyfication of Qianmen, have been a commercial breakthrough but a cultural disaster. Others offer an alternative model of how things could be, such as Nanluoguxiang, a short walk from Dali Courtyard (see p052) and packed with independent shops and bars, such as Salud (T 6402 5086), and the quirkier Wudaoying near the Lama Temple, which is filling up with fashion boutiques and cafés, including Vineyard (T 6402 7961).

17.30 Houhai

In the 13th century, the Mongol monarchs asked their engineers to hook up Beijing's much-loved lakes, aka Houhai, to the Grand Canal. During the Ming dynasty (1368-1644), the district was a fairground for the élite, while in more recent decades it has taken on a plebeian charm as a hangout for old men playing chess. Today, Houhai has morphed into a neon pub crawl. The trendsetter was the legendary No Name Bar (which opened in 2000 and is now closed), but then a swarm of lesser venues followed. The lakes themselves, however, retain their allure, so avoid the tacky bars that outnumber the gems and take a few drinks aboard a boat. Alternatively, cross over Di'anmen Xidajie and make your way to the old imperial garden of Beihai Park for a tour on the water around the dramatic White Dagoba.

20.00 Duck de Chine

You shouldn't leave Beijing without trying some duck. There are several eateries worth visiting – Da Dong (see p050), for example – but only one that combines top-notch food and a sleek, neo-industrial interior, all exposed beams and bare-brick walls. The restaurant is housed in one of the city's more successful regeneration projects: 1949 – The Hidden City, a small renovated factory complex reimagined by George Wang and opened in 2008. But the real draw is the duck. Here it's cooked over a wood fire for longer than normal, to get rid of the excess fat, and so must be pre-ordered. Enjoy with the traditional accompaniments of sesame bread, pancakes, spring onions and hoisin sauce. *1949 – The Hidden City, Courtyard Four, off Gongti Beilu, T 6501 1949, www.elite-concepts.com*

22.30 D Lounge

Beijing bar interiors don't get much better than this, possibly the capital's most beautiful drinking spot. Top cocktails, relaxed music, well-designed furniture and art all add atmosphere, but its best feature is the space itself. High ceilings, soaring arches and exposed brickwork lend an air of factory-meets-fashionista, while the white bar towers above it all, like a bacchanalian temple – more Gaudí than gaudy. Li Bo, who founded the bar with Warren Pang, conceived the design, which was executed by Sky Deng. Don't be put off by D Lounge's rather incongruous location, on a strip populated by students slamming cheap drinks – the crowd here is much more sophisticated.
Courtyard Four, Sanlitun Nanlu, T 6593 7710

URBAN LIFE
CAFÉS, RESTAURANTS, BARS AND NIGHTCLUBS

In terms of bars and restaurants, Beijing has some way to go before it can be compared with, say, London or New York. Nevertheless, this is a city that encourages people to play. Most of the action takes place either in the east, amid the perennial buzz of Sanlitun and Gongti, or among the hutongs and hipsters of Gulou.

Foodies can embark on a culinary journey across the country via Beijing's excellent regional restaurants. Standouts include the Shaanxi cuisine at Qin Tang Fu (53 & 69 Chaoyangmen Nanxiaojie, T 6559 8135), Sichuan at Chuan Ban (5 Gongyuantoutiao, T 6512 2277, ext 6101), Yunnan at Golden Peacock (16 Minzudaxue Beilu, T 6893 2030), the weekend dim sum at Lei Garden (3rd floor, Jinbao Tower, 89 Jinbaojie, T 8522 1212) and the dumplings at Din Tai Fung (24 Xinyuanxili Zhongjie, T 6462 4502).

The live-music scene is vibrant in Beijing. Seek out the local stars at Yu Gong Yi Shan (3-2 Zhangzi Zhonglu, T 6404 2711), Mao Livehouse (111 Gulou Dongdajie, T 6402 5080), Dos Kolegas (21 Liangmaqiao Lu, T 6436 8998) and D-22 (242 Chengfu Lu, T 6265 3177). Club kids flock to Mix (Workers' Stadium, Gongti Beilu, T 6530 2889), while fans of the absurd will enjoy Fubar (Workers' Stadium, Gongti Beilu, T 6546 8364), a speakeasy-style saloon accessed through a hot-dog shop. King of the local gay scene is Destination (7 Gongti Xilu, T 6552 8180).

For full addresses, see Resources.

Tiandi

When a restaurant is linked to a high-end furniture company, it's destined to look good. Beijing firm Domus Tiandi represents brands such as B&B Italia, as well as stocking classic Chinese antiques and accessories. The group also has two restaurants – one called Domus (T 8511 8015), the other, unsurprisingly, is Tiandi. Both are located on Nanchizi, a historic street that runs alongside the east wall of the Forbidden City, and both are beautifully designed. It's the latter, however, that has the food to match the style, although nearby Domus is worth visiting for an aperitif. Honouring thousands of years of tradition, this is imperial-style cooking, perfectly presented, which takes Chinese cuisine to the heights of fine dining. *140 Nanchizi Dajie, T 8511 5556, www.tiandiyijia.com*

Paper

In an area known for its scruffy boho cool, Paper stands defiant in its minimalism. Part of the Gulou empire of Cho Chong Gee, the Malaysian proprietor behind 3+1 Bedrooms (see p031), this place whispers measured simplicity – from its sparse façade, in stark contrast to the bustle and grit found along the rest of Gulou Dongdajie, to the all-white interior, broken only by the hardwood floors and a smattering of art. The food is in tune with the overall aesthetic: clean, contemporary Chinese cuisine, using lots of organic ingredients. Paper's healthy, modern fare is presented in a set menu, with an emphasis on vegetarian dishes.

138 Gulou Dongdajie, T 8401 5080, www.cafesambal.com

ROOMbeijing

In 2010, the capital's most-hyped opening was that of ROOMbeijing, a Brian McKenna venture. McKenna became the 21-year-old head chef at Michelin-starred restaurant Le Poussin in the UK before making his name in Beijing thanks to the molecular gastronomy he dished up at Blu Lobster (T 6841 2211 ext 6727) in the Shangri-La. ROOM leaves such culinary complexities behind. The vast space in the CBD features a mural by Brit Hugo Dalton, and pieces by rotating artists, such as the Beijing-based DAL, whose work has appeared in one of the two private dining rooms (above). The menu changes seasonally.

3rd floor, 301-302 Park Life Shopping Centre, Yintai Centre, 2 Jianguomenwai Dajie, T 8517 2033, www.room-beijing.com

Noodle Bar

Chinese food is still often regarded as convenient takeaway. But fast doesn't have to mean forlorn. Not when smart little places such as Noodle Bar prove that simple staples can be eaten with a degree of style. Set behind an unassuming door in the appropriately named The Hidden City – a former Sanlitun factory space turned dining destination – the venue has just 12 seats and three counters set around the open kitchen, which adds to the sense of intimacy. The menu is straightforward too, with a focus on beef noodle soup and some basic side dishes. Chefs prepare your order in front of you, adding a little theatre to the culinary proceedings.

1949 – The Hidden City, Courtyard Four, off Gongti Beilu, T 6501 1949, www.elite-concepts.com

Q Bar

Beijing can be a bizarre place sometimes. Take Q Bar – one of the city's best cocktail bars housed in one of its ugliest hotels. More bar on top of a hotel than hotel bar, Q has established itself as the go-to place for a martini or three. First-timers often arrive at the dull Eastern Inn hotel and assume they've come to the wrong place, but make your way past the check-in desk to the sixth floor and a cool lounge awaits. The terrace, and its sheltered alcoves, are particularly popular in the summer. This is still a benchmark bar in Beijing, but it faces a strong challenge from George's (T 6553 6299), launched by one of Q's original partners.
Eastern Inn, Sanlitun Nanlu/Gongti Nanlu, T 6595 9239, www.qbarbeijing.com

Maison Boulud

Most celebrated for his eponymous three-Michelin-starred restaurant in New York, French chef Daniel Boulud opened his first Beijing venue in what was once the American Embassy, in the neoclassical quadrangle off the south-east corner of Tiananmen Square. The Legation Quarter (or Ch'ien Men 23 as it has been rebranded) opened with a flourish in 2008, but as other tenants have fallen away, it is Maison Boulud that remains. The interiors by Gilles & Boissier are elegantly restrained, save perhaps for the Versailles-inspired mural, the service is faultless, the wine list superb and, of course, the French cuisine impeccable, thanks to Boulud's protégé Brian Reimer, who left NYC to run the Beijing restaurant. *Ch'ien Men 23, Qianmen Dongdajie, T 6559 9200, www.danielnyc.com*

Da Dong

Celebrity-chef culture is yet to grip the Middle Kingdom, but one name everyone knows locally is Da Dong, aka Beijing culinary hero Dong Zhenxiang, and the moniker of his three restaurants, all of which serve some of the very best *kaoya* (Peking duck) in town. Dong has more than 30 years of experience in the kitchen and has developed a method of cooking duck that results in crispy skin but juicy meat. He also applies molecular gastronomy to Chinese delicacies, creating dishes such as double-boiled bird's nest with rose jelly. Make a beeline for Da Dong's Nanxincang location, which Dong designed himself. It's part of a complex of old Ming dynasty granaries and is the hippest of the trio. *1st and 2nd floors, Nanxincang Guoji Dasha, 22 Dongsishitiao, T 5169 0329*

The Courtyard

When American attorney Handel Lee first visited China as a student in 1981, the nation was still opening up. Since then, he's gone on to oversee the development of Three on the Bund in Shanghai and the Legation Quarter in Beijing. But it was The Courtyard – his first venture, opened in 1997 – that cemented his reputation. A fine-dining East-West-fusion restaurant and art gallery in a renovated Qing dynasty building, this place was a real first for Beijing. The huge changes since then have led some to say this stalwart now lacks relevance. But in a city that moves so fast, The Courtyard should be celebrated for what it continues to deliver, not to mention the tables that overlook the moat around the Forbidden City.
95 Donghuamen Dajie, T 6526 8883,
www.courtyardbeijing.com

Dali Courtyard

Set in a small courtyard in an old hutong off Gulou Dongdajie, Dali serves cuisine from the south-western province of Yunnan. The chef will send out dishes to your table based on what is available on the day, while the RMB100 seasonal set menu means you don't need to speak or read Chinese to sample this delicious regional fare. Highlights have included delicately spiced mushrooms, mint-infused tofu and grilled tilapia with lemongrass. Book an alfresco table in summer or retreat to the warmth of the rustic rooms (above) in winter.

67 Xiaojingchang Hutong,
off Gulou Dongdajie, T 8404 1430,
www.dalicourtyard.com

Capital M

Melbourne-born restaurateur Michelle Garnaut's launch of M on the Bund in Shanghai in 1999 can be credited with kickstarting the revival of that city's waterfront. As for Capital M in Beijing, opened in 2009, few restaurants have been as keenly anticipated. The food is essentially solid modern European with a few Middle Eastern and North African dishes thrown in, but the most successful aspect of the venture is the striking interior, by Debra Little and Roger Hackworth, with a 50m hand-painted mural by Australian artist Michael Cartwright. Just metres from the old city gate near Tiananmen Square, Capital M is a must-visit while you're in Beijing, and the service is spot on.
3rd floor, 2 Qianmen Dajie, T 6702 2727, www.m-restaurantgroup.com/capitalm

Xiu
Designed by Tokyo-based firm Super Potato, the Park Hyatt's sixth-floor bar/lounge is a great spot for a summer cocktail. For a quieter crowd, slip away to China Bar on the 65th floor, Beijing's highest bar before Atmosphere (T 6505 2299) opened over the road on the 80th floor of the China World Summit Wing.
Park Hyatt, 2 Jianguomenwai Dajie, T 8567 1108, www.xiubeijing.com

Lan Club

Zhang Lan's restaurant chain South
Beauty started out with a simple concept:
sleek spaces for Beijing's bourgeoisie and
clean-cooked Sichuan spice. Then Zhang
and her son, Danny Wang, changed the
rules. For their next move, they hired
Philippe Starck to do the design – a first
for the capital. With a whole floor of a
mall to work with, the Frenchman went
to town. There are Baccarat chandeliers
and illuminated glass cabinets showcasing
vases, decanters and other objects. A
mirrored sushi and oyster bar shimmers
1940s-style, and the private rooms are
swathed in a splash-painted canvas.
4th floor, LG Twin Towers,
12 Jianguomenwai Dajie, T 5109 6012,
www.lan-global.com

Three Guizhou Men

Art is essential to this city. It's on display everywhere, from restaurants like The Courtyard (see p051) to hotels such as The Opposite House (see p022). Artist-run restaurants are a natural extension of this. They were born out of a desire to show friends' art, and often, for those from distant provinces, also provided the chance to bring a taste of home to the capital. Some look great, but the food lets things down, and vice versa. The most successful of these ventures is the Three Guizhou Men chain, set up by a trio from, yes, Guizhou. The best-looking of the bunch is the one in Wangjing (above), but the lively Gongti location (T 6551 8517) has a more lounge-like feel; the ribs served here are particularly recommended.
2nd floor, Nalisa Dasha, 1 Guangshun Nandajie, T 6470 7288

Ai Jiang Shan

With more than 100,000 Koreans living in Beijing (South Koreans are thought to outnumber any other expat community in the city), you won't have to look too hard to satisfy any cravings for *kimchi* and *banchan*. We suggest you head straight to Ai Jiang Shan – a class act, in terms of its décor and cuisine. The restaurant has locations in Chaoyang (T 8496 9511), handy if you're on your way to Dashanzi, and Haidian (above). Though the Haidian branch is a bit of a trek to the western edge of Universities, it's more refined. Ai Jiang Shan's prices are higher than at other Korean joints in town, but then none compare with the superior quality of the food here, the tasteful surroundings and the pleasant staff. *2 Zhengfusi Lu, T 5190 6655, www.aijiangshan.com*

Ichikura

A recent trend in Beijing's nightlife scene
is the whisky bar. The finest example
is Ichikura, which – as seems to be the
case with many of the city's best bars –
is hidden away and hard to find. In this
instance, you'll need to clamber up the
rickety stairs on the right-hand side of the
Chaoyang Theatre. Think of it as paying
homage to the acrobats who perform
there. Once inside, you'll find a softly lit,
sleek black bar that has more than
100 whiskies but just 12 seats, and
a wonderfully calm atmosphere. The
purposely small bar also allows Japanese
manager Koji Kuroki to provide some
of the finest service you'll find this side
of Tokyo. Watching him serve up a dram
of Yamazaki over a beautifully hand-
carved sphere of ice is a delight.
36 Dongsanhuan Beilu, T 6507 1107

Bei

This is one of the best dining experiences in town, thanks to Max Levy's culinary creativity and the stylish space created by Neri & Hu. Frank Gehry's 'Cloud' lamps over the sushi bar, and tableware from Spin (see p074) echo the discerning approach that makes its host, The Opposite House (see p022), such a joy.
Building 1, 11 Sanlitun Lu, T 6410 5230, www.beirestaurant.com

INSIDER'S GUIDE

LIN LIN, CREATIVE DIRECTOR, JELLYMON

The Chinese have their own term, *haigui* (sea turtle), for the reverse brain drain phenomenon – those who have lived abroad but then return to pursue career opportunities. Lin Lin left as a teenager and studied in Singapore and London, where she co-founded Jellymon, a creative agency with offices in Shanghai and Beijing, where she now lives. 'There's something majestic about this place,' she says.

For a quick lunch near her office, Lin Lin is a big fan of the home-style cooking at Tai Shu Xi (south of east gate, Tuanjiehu Park, T 8598 4766), where she recommends the vegetable hotpot and tofu dish *jia chang dou fu*. Her pick of the city's numerous hutong restaurants is Private Kitchen No 44 (44 Xiguan Hutong, T 6400 1280), for its fragrant spicy food from Guizhou. Middle 8th (8 Sanlitun Dong'erjie, T 6413 0629) and Apothecary (81 Sanlitun Beilu, T 5208 6040) are two of her other favourite spots; the former for its 'sophisticated Yunnanese food', the latter for 'Creole cuisine, which makes me love America'.

Apothecary's cocktails also make the venue her favourite weeknight bar, or she may drop by D Lounge (see p039), Mesh and Punk at The Opposite House (see p022), or the 'unpretentious and relaxed' Twilight (Jianwai Soho, 39 Dongsanhuan Zhonglu, T 5900 5376). After hours, Lin Lin likes to hang out at Yu Gong Yi Shan (see p040) for its live music and diverse crowd.

For full addresses, see Resources.

ARCHITOUR

A GUIDE TO BEIJING'S ICONIC BUILDINGS

The schizophrenic history of China's past 100 years is refracted through its architecture. The capital has served as a testing ground in the search for a modern Chinese style, some might say to its misfortune. A major drive for modernism came in the 1950s, with the 10th anniversary of the People's Republic in 1959 heralded by '10 great buildings' built in 10 months, including the Great Hall of the People (west of Tiananmen Square, T 6309 6935), Workers' Stadium (Gongti Beilu), National Museum of China (east of Tiananmen Square) and Beijing Railway Station (Beijing Huochezhan, Beijingzhanjie). Then three decades of skeletal tenements followed, broken only by Mao's mausoleum (see p066).

By the late 1980s, the Chinese Communist Party had a new MO: 'socialist market economy with Chinese characteristics'. Postmodern structures with imperial roofs and ornamental pagodas appeared. The city started looking up, with towers such as the CITIC Building (19 Jianguomenwai Dajie) and Capital Mansion (6 Xinyuan Nanlu) piercing the horizontal skyline.

The Olympics saw Beijing embrace the future, with ambitious if controversial architecture such as the National Stadium (see p014), CCTV Building (see p010) and, more recently, Zaha Hadid's planned Galaxy Soho complex. All epitomise the bold, self-confident city that hits you as soon as you arrive in Foster + Partners' Terminal 3. *For full addresses, see Resources.*

Linked Hybrid

While everyone was obsessing over the National Stadium (see p014), Steven Holl Architects was quietly getting on with the city's other cutting-edge development. Completed in 2009, Linked Hybrid is an eight-tower mixed-use complex that has transformed a corner of the city (where the Second Ring Road meets the Airport Expressway) into a dynamic urban space. The towers are linked on their upper floors by a series of bridges, containing galleries, eateries and even a pool, which hover above a large pond. One of Beijing's first green residential projects, Linked Hybrid draws on a geothermal water source to control the heating and cooling systems. Visit the art-house cinema, Broadway Cinematheque (T 8438 8258), to experience this 'open city within a city'.
Grand Moma, 1 Xiangheyuan Lu

Chairman Mao Memorial Hall
Built in just six months by the citizens of
Beijing, and opened in 1977, exactly one
year after his death, Mao's mausoleum
symbolically used material from all over
the country. It was also placed directly
on the city's central axis in Tiananmen
Square, with its north-facing entrance
intentionally blocking the old imperial
sight line from the Forbidden City.
South Tiananmen Square, T 6513 1130

NCPA

When French architect Paul Andreu won the 1998-99 competition to fill the 'big pit' beside the Great Hall of the People (see p064), critics lampooned his bubble of glass and titanium as everything from a duck egg to a dung pile. But defenders saw an iota of Chinese thinking in its circle-in-square geometry. Regardless, the verdict on the 2007 National Centre for the Performing Arts (NCPA), aka the Egg, is now in, and it's safe to say that Andreu has indeed created an iconic building that's become part of the fabric of the city and a cultural locomotive to boot. The venue regularly hosts world-class classical music, allowing visitors to move from Mao to Mozart in moments. *2 Xichang'anjie, T 6655 0000, www.chncpa.org*

Dongbianmen Watchtower
In 2002, the city excavated the Ming
dynasty wall next to this tower, razing a
block of rundown homes and reclaiming
thousands of original bricks. The Ming
Dynasty City Wall Relics Park (T 6527
0574) was duly built. Lit up at night,
it's an arresting sight. Visit the Red Gate
Gallery (T 6525 1005) inside the tower.
Chongwenmen Dongdajie/
Jianguomen Nandajie

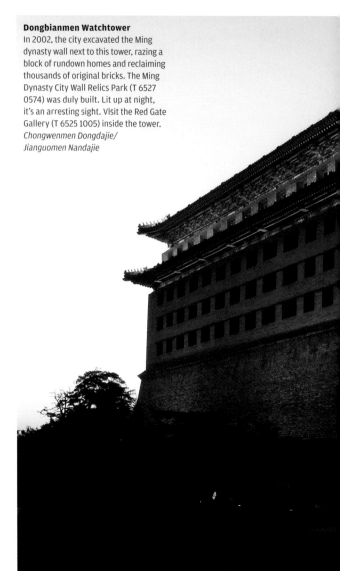

SHOPPING

THE BEST RETAIL THERAPY AND WHAT TO BUY

It should come as no surprise that some of the main shopping attractions for many visitors to the 'factory of the world' are the huge markets selling cheap goods – everything from 'luxury' labels to kitsch memorabilia. In an effort to clean things up, that infamous bazaar of ersatz brand names, Silk Street (8 Xiushui Dongjie, T 5169 9003), was moved indoors in 2005. 'Cheaper, cheaper' China also lives on at Hongqiao market (46 Tiantan Donglu, T 6713 3354), near the Temple of Heaven (see p033), where the gems on offer include dyed freshwater pearls. Not so far from here is the fun Panjiayuan fleamarket (Panjiayuanqiao, T 6775 2405). The 'antiques' are rarely so, but charming curios abound. Continuing the theme in Sanlitun is the Yashow clothing market (58 Gongti Beilu, T 6415 1726), where haggling is de rigueur.

But there is more to the capital than bargain-hunting in the bazaars. The rise of the mall is unstoppable. If you're looking for the big brands, visit Joy City (131 Xidan Beidajie, T 5833 0000), where you should check out Arrtco (T 5971 6186), or Sanlitun Village (see p082). For independent boutiques, head to Nali Patio (81 Sanlitun Lu). Your best bet for unearthing unique items is to scour Gulou Dongdajie, home of Spoon House (opposite), and Nanluoguxiang. Start with Grifted (28 Nanluoguxiang, T 6402 0409) and Bye Bye Disco (38-2 Nanluoguxiang, T 6402 5581).
For full addresses, see Resources.

Spoon House

Gulou Dongdajie is a great street on which to while away an afternoon. Lined with one-off stores, it offers everything from guitar shops to an entire outlet dedicated to the Japanese manga cat Doraemon. One of the more interesting shops is Spoon House. It's not much to look at – simple shelves line whitewashed walls in a fairly cramped space – but it is packed with quirky Chinese designs.

Among our picks are these Li Lei and Han Meimei notebooks (above), RMB49 for three, which feature characters from an old textbook used by children learning English. The familiar graphics are accompanied by cheeky and incongruous phrases, such as 'Treat the sex relationship right' and 'You are omnipotent'.
211 Gulou Dongdajie, T 6400 6419, www.spoonhouse.cn

Spin Ceramics
Created by master ceramicists from
Hong Kong and Jingdezhen, China's
legendary repository of porcelain,
Spin's creations are superb. The pieces
evoke an aesthetic derived from nature;
jars drip with red glaze, and tea and
sake sets bear the patina of ground
tofu. The only things less showy than
the ceramics are the reasonable prices.
6 Fangyuan Xilu, T 6437 8649

Liu + de Biolley

Harrison Liu is an actor/director turned designer whose furniture has been picked up by one of China's largest stores, Qumei; it's also sold internationally. Jehanne de Biolley is a jeweller who has created pieces for the Belgian monarchy. The married couple, one of the city's most creative partnerships, have lent their talents to everything from filmmaking to hotel design. Their impressive home, in what used to be the library of a Ming dynasty temple, is also their studio and a shop. Liu makes contemporary furniture inspired by imperial culture; de Biolley's couture ranges from bold made-to-order jewellery to hand-woven silk decorated with beads. Call to make an appointment and they will talk you through their work. *61 Dashiqiao Hutong, T 139 0124 6125 (Liu); T 139 0120 6068 (de Biolley)*

O Gallery
The industrial wasteland next to the
Dashanzi Art District (see p034) is best
known as a location for fashion shoots,
but design showroom O Gallery is
changing that. Set up by The Alliance
collective, it presents Western and
Chinese designers, such as Liu Feng's PEP
Art + Design and Song Tao's Self-Made.
*4 Jiuxianqiao Lu, 751 District,
T 8459 9676, www.o-gallery.com*

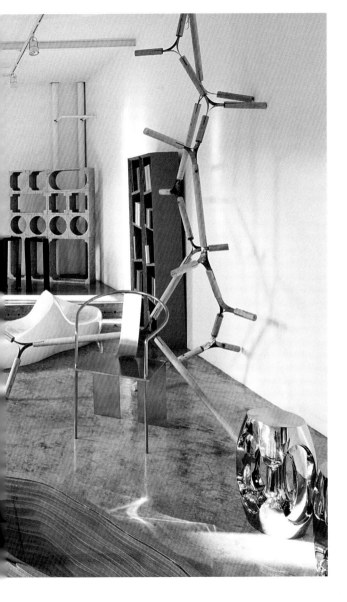

Dong Liang

This stripped-down showroom for local fashion and accessories designers is all about promoting fresh talent. Situated on the up-and-coming Wudaoying, which, thanks to its cafés, bars and boutiques is being touted as the 'next Nanluoguxiang', Dong Liang is a good example of what happens when the hutongs become hip. The bare, rough-edged interior – brick walls, wooden beams and a grey stone floor – is the right backdrop for a tight edit of the rising stars of China's fast-developing fashion scene. Look out for Vega Wang, who has previously worked at Alexander McQueen and Vivienne Westwood.
26 Wudaoying Hutong, T 8404 7648

Lost & Found

You may not immediately associate discarded government-issue chairs with retro chic, but you may change your mind after a visit to this Gulou store, hidden away down a hutong near the Lama Temple. Shan Shan, Paul Gelinas and Xiao Mao, the trio behind the venture, collect Mao-era furniture, which they renovate and refashion as limited-edition pieces. They also salvage all sorts of other classic items, from battered leather bags to phones, which they clean up and sell on. Lost & Found also collaborates with China's oldest functioning thermos factory to produce some very cool reissued flasks.
42 Guozijianjie, T 6401 1855.
www.lost-and-found.cn

Chang & Biörck

Located in Sanlitun Village, Sino-Scandi home accessories outlet Chang & Biörck occupies a tiny space that does justice to the word 'compact'. Founded by India Chang and Eva Biörck, it sells covetable tableware, cushion covers and lamps that fuse Chinese and Scandinavian materials and motifs. Its host, the Village mall, is a Kengo Kuma-designed complex incorporating international flagships for Apple, Adidas and the like. It's almost impossible to overstate the impact that Sanlitun Village has had on the area – much like Kuma's wonderful hotel, The Opposite House (see p022).
Unit S02-19A, Sanlitun Village, Sanlitun Lu, T 8400 2296, www.changbiorck.com

Fei Space

Artist and ceramicist Lin Jing's work has sold at 10 Corso Como in Milan and has been exhibited at the V&A in London. Back in Beijing, she has transformed her home in Dashanzi into an independent boutique, creating one of the most original shops in town. Fei Space is the place locals come to pick up international labels hard to find on the Mainland, while visitors may be more interested in the Chinese fashion designers stocked here, including Zhang Da and Qiu Hao. Then, of course, there's Lin Jing's sculptural tableware – not to be missed.
B-01, 4 Jiuxianqiao Lu,
Dashanzi Art District, T 5978 9580

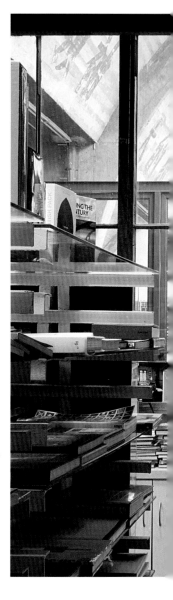

Timezone 8 Bookshop
Contemporary Chinese art found one
of its earliest promoters in Texan Robert
Bernell, who created the respected
online magazine chinese-art.com in
1998, followed by the publishing house
Timezone 8 Art Books. Bernell's bookshop
found a natural home at the epicentre
of the emerging scene in 798. Housed
in what was once a factory canteen, in a
space designed by architects Mary-Ann
Ray and Robert Mangurian, the shop stocks
a fine list of titles on the Chinese visual
arts, including Timezone 8's own English-
language publications, which cover art,
architecture, photography and design.
The grassroots scene may have shifted
away from here, but the store still acts
as a hub, hosting talks, book launches
and film nights in English and Chinese.
4 Jiuxianqiao Lu, Dashanzi Art District,
T 8456 0336

SPORTS AND SPAS

WORK OUT, CHILL OUT OR JUST WATCH

It's somewhat ironic that a city that placed such importance on the Olympics is not a particularly sporty place. Sydney this is not, and the closest people get to a surf before work is a stressful cycle through Beijing's traffic-heavy streets. Pollution is a serious problem and the city air is frequently terrible. Official statistics aren't necessary when you can see the smog with your own eyes; smokers joke that the habit helps their lungs adapt.

For those who insist on pounding the pavements – perhaps one of the brave souls in training for the annual Great Wall Marathon in May – the best time to run on the utterly flat streets is dawn. Better still are the parks, which provide scenery but aren't really big enough to avoid doing laps. A 5km stretch around Houhai is a good morning option, and jogging is a great way to see the Summer Palace, Peking University and Tsinghua University.

The city's spas are a more inviting prospect. Beijingers love to be pampered and a foot massage or a back rub is never far away; Dragonfly (www.dragonfly.net.cn), Oriental Taipan Massage & Spa (www.taipan.com.cn) and Bodhi (www.bodhi.com.cn) each have salons dotted across town. New yoga studios open all the time, but aficionados should try the established Yoga Yard (17 Gongti Beilu, T 6413 0774) and Om Yoga 42° (Lido Apartment Building, T 6437 8810), or the expanding Yogi Yoga chain (en.yogiyoga.cn). *For full addresses, see Resources.*

Milun School of Traditional Kungfu

Callisthenics and low-resistance exercise apparatus reign in the parks, but to pick up time-honoured kung fu moves, one must cultivate ties with a master. The Milun School is based in a double courtyard complex in Wangfujing, and instructors also run one-on-one tutorials in Ritan Park. The centre emphasises a balance between defence, conditioning and philosophy. Courses range from the Taoist 'internal' arts of 'form and intention' to 'external' styles, such as Sanda (Chinese kick-boxing). Master Zhang Shengli has moonlighted at the Beijing Police Academy, while his Chicagoan protégée, Sabrina Cohen, runs Academic Explorers (T 137 1876 4084), which provides training in kung fu and Mandarin tailored to individual needs. *33 Xitangzi Hutong, T 138 1170 6568, www.kungfuinchina.com*

Bath House Residence

Soon after opening in May 2009, Jin R's
Bath House Residence at the Green T
House Living complex won a Wallpaper*
Design Award. Those familiar with her
Green T House restaurant (T 6552 8310)
in Sanlitun will have an inkling of what to
expect from the imperial-inspired haven.
A vast, minimalist retreat in the north-
eastern suburbs, the complex comprises
a fine-dining restaurant, teahouse, gallery,
events space and gardens, as well as this
ultra-chic spa, which takes its cue from
the bathhouse of a concubine to a Tang
dynasty emperor. Whether you opt for the
10-hand massage or a dip in the rooftop
jacuzzi, or spend the night in one of the
loft bedrooms, you'll soon discover there's
nowhere else quite like this in Beijing.
*318 Cuigezhuang Xiang, Hegezhuang
Cun, T 6434 2519, www.green-t-house.com*

Park Life Fitness

Serious swimmers should head to Houhai and join the Beijingers taking a dip in the lakes (they even cut a lane through the ice in winter). But for something more genteel, visit the Park Hyatt gym, designed by Super Potato. The 25m pool (pictured) on the sixth floor of the hotel has a double-height glazed roof, lending it a refreshing sense of light and space. There are two whirlpools and an outdoor terrace, while the fitness centre, also covered by an arched roof, runs tai chi and yoga classes. There is also Tian Spa, on the 59th and 60th floors of the hotel. Both spa areas offer Chinese medicinal treatments, such as *ba guan* cupping, *tuina* and meridian massages.
Park Hyatt, 2 Jianguomenwai Dajie, T 8567 1111, www.beijing.park.hyatt.com

Zenspa

This place is a diamond in the rough of the city's construction-supplies district. Its courtyard confines are feng shui'd to the hilt and highlighted by floating orchids and coronas of light. The private rooms, alas, place less emphasis on luxury – Zenspa is a serious treatment clinic. The therapists have travelled far and wide to study, returning to impart their knowledge. The four-and-a-half-hour

Detox package, which includes a sea-salt scrub, herbal bath, aromatherapy massage and facial, doesn't come cheap, though discounts are sometimes available. *House 1, 8a Xiaowuji Lu, T 8731 2530, www.zenspa.com.cn*

ESCAPES

WHERE TO GO IF YOU WANT TO LEAVE TOWN

'He who hasn't climbed the Great Wall is not a real man,' Mao once stated. But touristy parts such as Badaling are for the softest of travellers. By contrast, the hills, temples, tombs and ruins that surround Beijing have drawn swelling numbers of weekend warriors on excursions in recent years.

It is history, however, that is Greater Beijing's finest feature. At Zhoukoudian, it goes back 500,000 years to our early evolution, thanks to the discovery of Peking Man at what is now a UNESCO World Heritage Site. Moving forward to imperial times, the Ming dynasty tombs can be combined with a trip to the Great Wall (opposite). Then there is the slightly less strenuous option of a picnic and overnight stay at the hillside hamlet of Cuandixia, where some villagers still live in 400-year-old earth-and-stone dwellings. Around four hours from the capital by train is Chengde (not to be confused with Chengdu), where the great Qing emperors decamped – think of it as the Summer Palace on steroids.

If you really want to connect with China's past, try the ancient walled town of Pingyao in Shanxi Province, south-west of Beijing. The sleepy preserve was a cutting-edge banking capital during the Qing dynasty (1644-1912). This evocative atmosphere comes with modern comfort at boutique hotel Jing's Residence (16 East Avenue, T 0354 584 1000), a former silk merchant's house.
For full addresses, see Resources.

Commune by the Great Wall

About an hour north-west of the city, China's imperial rulers found a serene resting spot at what is now called Shisanling (Thirteen Tombs) after the 13 Ming emperors buried in this peaceful valley. Another 25km to the north-east lies the Huanghuacheng (Yellow Flower City) section of the Great Wall, where the crumbling Ming dynasty masonry bottoms out at a reservoir. Hike with caution: the new élite's weekend homes are dotted below. The ideal base camp is Commune by the Great Wall, 30km to the north-west of the mausoleums. Its stand-alone villas, including the Kengo Kuma-designed Bamboo House (above) and Antonio Ochoa's Cantilever House (overleaf), have won developer SOHO China several awards. *Exit 53, G6 Highway, T 8118 1888, www.commune.com.cn*

Cantilever House, Commune by the Great Wall

Songzhuang Art Village

The villages north and east of Beijing have proved as important to China's art scene as the French countryside was to the Impressionists. Yet none possess the scale, folklore or staying power of Songzhuang, 30km east of the capital. When this enclave formed in the mid-1990s, anti-establishment figures had to move constantly to dodge the police. But attitudes have changed so much that now the local government sponsors the Songzhuang Art Festival and a museum. Past residents include the performance artist Zhang Huan and the cynical realists Yue Minjun and Fang Lijun. Today, around 4,000 artists are based here and the galleries are too numerous to list, but Artist Village Gallery (pictured, T 6959 8343) has one of the largest exhibition spaces.

Xiangshan
Beijingers love to hike the paths of
Xiangshan (Fragrant Hills) up to Incense
Burner Peak, where they can gape at
their smoggy city some 25km away.
Other sights here include Mao's former
home, near IM Pei's Fragrant Hill Hotel
(T 6259 1166), and the Temple of Azure
Clouds to the north. The Sculpting In
Time café (T 8529 0040) by Xiangshan's
east gate makes a scenic pitstop.

NOTES
SKETCHES AND MEMOS

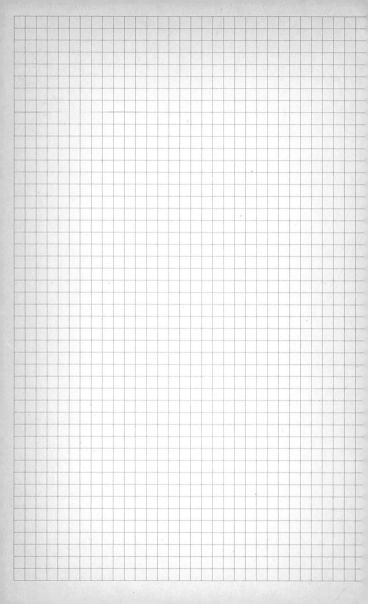

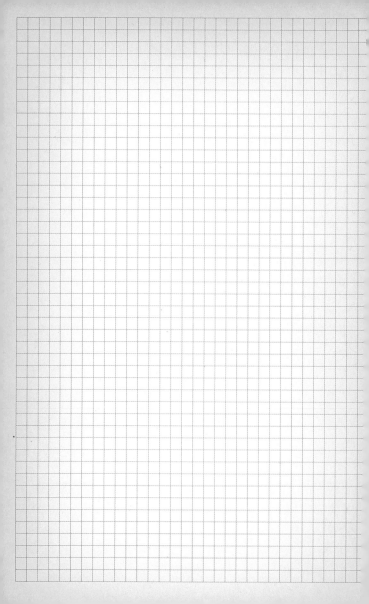

RESOURCES
CITY GUIDE DIRECTORY

HOTELS

ADDRESSES AND ROOM RATES

Aman at Summer Palace 017
Room rates:
double, from RMB4,290;
Imperial Suite, from RMB29,629
1 Gongmenqianjie
Summer Palace
T 5987 9999
www.amanresorts.com

China World Hotel 025
Room rates:
double, RMB1,898;
Beijing Suite, RMB46,000
China World Trade Center
1 Jianguomenwai Dajie
T 6505 2266
www.shangri-la.com

Commune by the Great Wall 097
Room rates:
double, from RMB2,173;
Cantilever House, from RMB13,524
Exit 53
G6 Highway
T 8118 1888
www.commune.com.cn

The Emperor 028
Room rates:
double, from RMB969;
Emperor Suite, from RMB5,299
33 Qiheloujie
T 6526 5566
www.theemperor.com.cn

Fragrant Hill Hotel 102
Room rates:
double, RMB960
Haidian district
Fragrant Hill Park
T 6259 1166
www.xsfd.com

The Great Wall Sheraton 016
Room rates:
double, RMB1,587
10 Dongsanhuan Beilu
T 6590 5566
www.sheraton.com.cn/beijing

Hotel Côté Cour 026
Room rates:
double, from RMB1,228
70 Yanyue Hutong
T 6523 7981
www.hotelcotecourbj.com

Hotel G 016
Room rates:
double, from RMB1,136
A7 Gongti Xilu
T 6552 3600
www.hotel-g.com

Hotel Kapok 016
Room rates:
double, from RMB800
16 Donghuamen Dajie
T 6525 9988
www.hotelkapok.com

Jing's Residence 096
Room rates:
double, RMB1,265
16 East Avenue
T 0354 584 1000

The Opposite House 022
Room rates:
double, from RMB2,242
The Penthouse, on request
11 Sanlitun Lu
T 6417 6688
www.theoppositehouse.com

Raffles Hotel 024
  Room rates:
  double, RMB2,288;
  Landmark Suite, RMB4,485
  33 Dongchang'anjie
  T 6526 3388
  www.beijing.raffles.com
Red Capital Residence 030
  Room rates:
  double, RMB1,380;
  Author Suite, from RMB978;
  The Chairman Suite, from RMB1,380
  9 Dongsi Liutiao
  T 8403 5308
  www.redcapitalclub.com.cn
3+1 Bedrooms 031
  Room rates:
  double, from RMB1,360;
  Jade Suite, from RMB2,380
  17 Zhangwang Hutong
  Off Jiugulou Dajie
  T 6404 7030
  www.3plus1bedrooms.com
Yi House 020
  Room rates:
  double, from RMB1,115;
  deluxe suite, from RMB2,875
  2 Jiuxianqiao Lu
  T 6436 1818
  www.yi-house.com

WALLPAPER* CITY GUIDES

Editorial Director
Richard Cook

Art Director
Loran Stosskopf

Editor
Rachael Moloney

Author
Adrian Sandiford

Consultant City Editor
Jonathan Ansfield

Deputy Editor
Jeremy Case

Managing Editor
Jessica Diamond

Designer
Lara Collins

Map Illustrator
Russell Bell

Photography Editor
Sophie Corben

Photography Assistant
Robin Key

Sub-Editors
Vanessa Harriss
Greg Hughes
Vicky McGinlay

Editorial Assistant
Ella Marshall

Interns
Ayse Koklu
Kerry Norwood

**Wallpaper* Group
Editor-in-Chief**
Tony Chambers

Publishing Director
Gord Ray

Wallpaper* ® is a
registered trademark
of IPC Media Limited

First published 2007
Second edition (revised
and updated) 2011
© 2007 and 2011 IPC
Media Limited

ISBN 978 0 7148 6092 3

PHAIDON

Phaidon Press Limited
Regent's Wharf
All Saints Street
London N1 9PA

Phaidon Press Inc
180 Varick Street
New York, NY 10014

Phaidon® is a registered
trademark of Phaidon
Press Limited

www.phaidon.com

A CIP Catalogue record for
this book is available from
the British Library.

All prices are correct at
time of going to press,
but are subject to change.

Printed in China

PHOTOGRAPHERS

Iwan Baan
National Stadium,
pp014-015

OJPhotos/Alamy
Temple of Heaven, p033

Eric Gregory Powell
Aman at Summer Palace,
p017, pp018-019
Yi House, p020, p021
UCCA, pp034-035
Duck de Chine, p038
D Lounge, p039
Tiandi, p041
Paper, pp042-043
ROOMbeijing, p044
Noodle Bar, p045
Q Bar, p046, p047
Maison Boulud,
pp048-049
Da Dong, p050
The Courtyard, p051
Dali Courtyard, p052
Xiu, pp054-055
Three Guizhou Men, p057
Ai Jiang Shan, p058
Ichikura, p059
Lin Lin, p063
Chairman Mao Memorial
Hall, pp066-067
Liu + de Biolley,
pp076-077

O Gallery, pp078-079
Dong Liang, p080
Lost & Found, p081
Chang & Biorck,
pp082-083
Fei Space, p084, p085

Andrew Rowat
CCTV Building, pp010-011
Green T House Living &
Bath House Residence,
pp090-091

Oak Taylor-Smith
Beijing city view,
inside front cover
Forbidden City, pp012-013
Red Capital
Residence, p030
Hutong tour, p036
Houhai, p037
Lan Club, p056
NCPA, pp068-069
Dongbianmen Watchtower,
pp070-071
Spin Ceramics, pp074-075
798, pp086-087
Milun School of Traditional
Kung Fu, p089
Xiangshan, pp102-103

Tony Law
Hotel Côté Cour,
p026, p027
The Emperor, p028, p029
3+1 Bedrooms, p031
Park Life Fitness,
pp092-093

Peartree Digital
Notebooks from
Spoon House, p073

Jonathan de Villiers
Linked Hybrid, p065

BEIJING

A COLOUR-CODED GUIDE TO THE HOT 'HOODS

EAST SIDE
Beijing's CBD is rising fast; view the range of glass and steel from the peaceful Ritan Park

UNIVERSITIES
Campus life dominates the north-west, which teems with tech geeks and internet cafés

TIANANMEN
Hopscotch through China's past, from the Forbidden City to Chairman Mao's memorial

GULOU
The disappearing hutongs still draw the hip crowd to their eateries, bars and boutiques

OLD CITY
Seek out the gems of the emperor's old domain before modernisation swallows them up

SANLITUN
Switching from seedy to swanky, this area remains the heart of Beijing's nightlife scene

For a full description of each neighbourhood, see the Introduction.
Featured venues are colour-coded, according to the district in which they are located.